FLORENCE

BONECHI EDITORE - FIRENZE

VIA DEI RUSTICI, 5

The " Explosion of the Cart " which takes place each year on
Easter Sunday in Piazza San Giovanni.

The Cathedral (S. Maria del Fiore)

The grandiose building was started by Arnolfo di Cambio in 1296, having the commission from the Republic to carry out the work « with the most high and sumptuous magnificence so that it is impossible to make it either better or more beautiful with the industry and power of man », in the place where the church of Santa Reparata, the cathedral of Florence had been, and facing San Giovanni. On the death of Arnolfo, which came about in 1302, the works were interrupted and taken over in 1357 under the direction of Giotto, who was already supervising the realisation of the belltower. He died in 1337, and the work suffered a slowing down and from 1357 to 1364 the Cathedral Works Committee entrusted the direction to Lapo Ghini and Francesco Talenti, committing them with a project which was more grandiose than that of Arnolfo. Finally, in 1366 a definite plan was submitted by four architects and the construction continued with an easier rythm. In 1378 the vault of the middle nave were already completed, and from 1380 to 1421 the empore and the tambour of the dome were constructed. In 1436 Pope Eugenius IV solemnly consecrated the temple, dedicating to Santa Maria del Fiore. The facade was erected by the Florentine architect Emilio de Fabris who was inspired by Florentine Gothic style, continuing the construction from 1871 to 1883 and decorating it with statues carried out by contemporary artists.

The Cathedral's facing in marble of three colors: white marble from Carrara, green from Prato, and red from the Maremma region. On the **façade** inside the niches are 12 statues of the Apostles, with the Virgin and Child in the center. On either side of the portals are four statues representing the bishops who blessed the first stone, the first pier, and the façade; the third to the left is Pope Eugene IV who consecrated the church.

In the photo above, **interior of the Duomo.** Divided into three naves by composite pillars, which support the arches and pointed Gothic vaults, it is a typical example of Florentine Gothic architecture. In the photo below, a partial view of the **crypt** of the ancient **Cathedral of Santa Reparata**, recently brought to light by excavations; in the foreground are funeral stones. On the next page, the « **Pietà** » by Michelangelo which stands in the Duomo and which the artist sculpted to be placed on his tomb.

The Dome. - During the construction of the Cathedral in 1418, a competition was announced for the building of the dome, won by Filippo Brunelleschi who carried out the marvellous architectural masterpiece from 1420 to 1434, and it is the admiration of the world today. Michelangelo himself was inspired by this masterpiece to construct the dome of St. Peter's in Rome. It is 91 metres high without the lantern, 114 with the lantern and 45,52 metres in diameter above the tambour. From the terrace of the parapet walk, 107 metres above ground, one can enjoy a vast and very beautiful panorama.

Giotto's Belltower. - 81,75 metres high even today it remains of a beauty that has no competitors in all the world, after more than half a millennium since its construction. In 1334, at the invitation of the Signoria, Giotto presented his designs and the foundations of the colossal work, and the building was started in July of the same year. Unfortunately, it was three years to the day after this that Giotto died and the work was continued until 1348 by Andrea Pisano and finished off by Francesco Talenti in 1359. However, both of them scrupulously followed the designs of the great master, except for the terminal spire which was never constructed and would have added another thirdy metres or so to height of the belltower. A very lovely panorama of the city and the hills that surround it can be enjoyed from the terrace at which one arrives after having climbed 414 steps.

The Baptistery

This is one of the oldest buildings in Florence, one which Dante remembers, calling it « my lovely San Giovanni », the place where he was baptised. Judged earlier on to be a construction of the V century, it is now held to be a Romanesque construction of the XI-XII century, built on the remains of a paleochristian monument where the remains of a Roman construction were found in the foundations. It is an example of Tuscan Romanesque architecture on an octagonal plan with coloured marbles, and surrounded by a double order of pilasters which support the arches. The covering of the dome is hidden by an attic (XIII century). It was consacrated to St. John the Baptist and was cathedral of Florence until 1128. The three entrance doors which are of exceptional interest, are placed according to the cardinal points.

Lorenzo Ghiberti

Vittorio Ghiberti

Lorenzo Ghiberti's « Door of Paradise » took 27 years to complete (1425-1452). Old and New Testament scenes are represented in the panels.

10

INTERIOR OF THE BAPTISTRY - View of the interior
of the Baptistry and the mosaics of the Cupola.

CATHEDRAL MUSEUM - One of the Museum's rooms.

Two panels of Giotto's Bell-Tower
now in the Cathedral Museum.

14

Medici Chapel

Right, Piazza Madonna degli Aldobrandini, where the entrance of the Medici Chapels is situated. Below, the **New Sacristy,** by Michelangelo (1520-33) in the Medici Chapels. - The great Michelangelo wanted to give a grandiose and solemn feeling in the architectural parts as much as the sculptural parts. Here the three famous tombs, of which only two have been completely finished, can be found. Michelangelo sculpted only the Madonna and Child for the unfinished one. This magnificent masterpiece shows us Michelangelo as an architect as well as a sculptor. One could say that they both amount to the same thing as one cannot admire each individual work on its own, but must look at them as an inseparable whole, where architecture and sculpture are based and completed by one another. The quadrangular room with the powerful dome is full of movement and every architectural element shows up the plastic energy of the mass.

The Tomb of Giuliano Duke of Nemours, by Michelangelo. Giuliano is represented seated and wearing the armour and staff of command, a symbol of action; at his feet are the two symbolic figures that represent Day and Night.

The Night.

The Day.

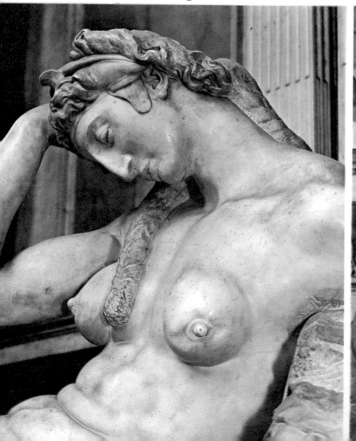

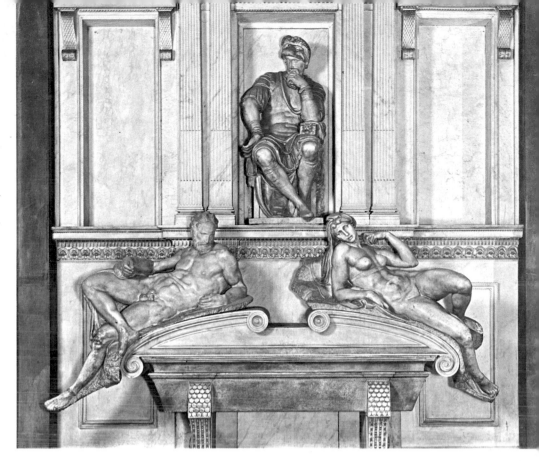

The Tomb of **Lorenzo Duke of Urbino,** by Michelangelo. The Duke of Urbino, grandson of Lorenzo the Magnificent, is represented in a thoughtful pose with two figures on the sarcophagus symbolising Dawn und Dusk.

The Dusk.

The Dawn.

The Chapel of the Princes in the Medici Chapels.
- The construction of this wonderful building was started in 1604 by Matteo Nigetti from a design by Prince Giovanni de' Medici, who wished to have the sepulchre of the Medici family constructed here and worthy of their power and riches. In fact is was called the chapel of the Princes. The walls are completely covered in precious marbles, finely prepared « pietra dura » (hard stone) and gilded bronzes. The six porphyry sarcophagi belong to the Medici grand dukes from Cosimo I to Cosimo III. The bronze statues are by Pietro Tacca (XVII century).

18

PIAZZA SAN LORENZO —
At the centre of the popular market (which dates from 1870 when Florence was the capital of Italy) is the statue of Giovanni delle Bande Nere, done by Baccio Bandinelli in 1540. The church was originally dedicated to San Lorenzo in 393 by St. Ambrose, bishop of Milan, and for this reason it is also known as the Ambrosian Basilica. It assumed its present form in 1423 when rebuilt by Brunelleschi, commissioned by Giovanni di Bicci de' Medici. Later Michelangelo built the Chapels containing the Medici tombs and the library, and finished the inside of the church's facade. He designed the outside of the facade but this work was never carried out.

Piazza della Signoria. This is Florence's most famous and beautiful square, dominated by the noble Palazzo Vecchio (also called the Palazzo della Signoria), and the Loggia dei Lanzi. Around it are many other old buildings, and it contains the Fountain of Neptune and numerous celebrated statues. It was here, over a period of centuries, that the great political and historical events of the city took place, and the square has become something of a symbol of the internal struggles in Florence, the establishment of its international prestige and power, and the civilisation and culture which it gave to the world.

Equestrian monument of the Grand Duke Cosimo I de' Medici, the work of Giambologna in 1594, on the base are three bass reliefs with significative episodes from the life of the Grand Duke.

Fontana di Piazza, by Bartolomeo Ammannati (1563-75). The fountain is dominated by the huge white statue of Neptune, an unfortunate work called by the Florentines « il Biancone » (Big White man). Much more worthy of note are the bronze statues which adorn the basin of the fountain, depicting naiads and satyrs and created by Ammannati and other artists, among them Giambologna.

The Loggia of the Signoria

A rare example of late Gothic work with early Renaissance warnings.
It was also called the **Loggia of the Lanzi** because the Lanzichenecchi were stationed here in the XVI century as a guard for Cosimo I, and it was also given the name of the **Loggia dell'Orcagna**, following the supposed design by the artist. The construction was actually owed to the same architects who were in charge of the construction of the Cathedral, in other words: Benci di Cione, Simone di Francesco Talenti and others from 1376 to 1382, and was built for the elections and proclamations of the Priors and the Gonfalonier as well as other cerimonies of the Signoria. The masterpieces of sculpture underneath the loggia, belonging to various periods, make a marvellous open-air museum.

« **Perseus** » by Benvenuto Cellini

« **The Rape of the Sabine Women** » by Giambologna

Palazzo Vecchio

It represents the principal architectural monument in Florence and one of the most significant mediaeval public palaces in Italy. It rises up, majestic and severe in its power, with its tower (94 metres high) which is thrown straight up from the facade, with great clarity of construction, which gives a particular character of elegance to the whole building. According to tradition it was constructed by the genius Arnolfo di Cambio from 1298 to 1314, using the castle of the Counts Guidi di Poppi as a model, but this attribution has not been substantiated by any document. The original construction was a great parallelepiped in rough rustic work with very beautiful Gothic two lighted windows on two floors and crowned by a great parapet walk with esparto battlementing. In the front, the tower that goes by the name of Arnolfo rises up on a rectangular design, erected laterally because it was constructed on the pre-existing one of the Foraboschi, with battlemented double bow windows.

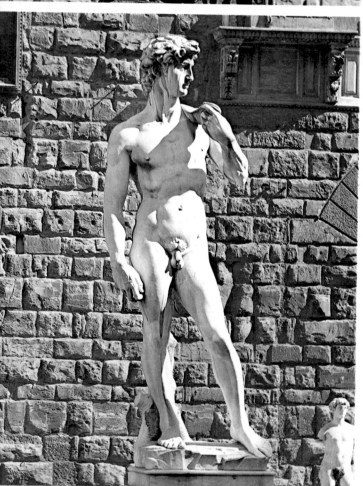

On the page at left: above, the **Courtyard of the Palazzo Vecchio**, designed by Michelozzo. The frescoes on the walls are by Vasari, and the basin on the fountain in the centre is by Battista del Tadda. The « Winged Boy with a Fish » is a copy of the original by Verrocchio. In the photograph below, the **Hall of the Five Hundred** designed by Il Cronaca; on its walls are frescoes by Vasari, who also did the paintings on the ceiling with their carved, gilded frames.

In the photo above left, « **The Victory of the Spirit over Brute Force** », a marble group done by Michelangelo in 1525 which stands in the central niche of the end wall of the Hall of the Five Hundred. On the right, one of the six statues along the walls depicting « **The Labours of Hercules** », by Vincenzo de' Rossi

THE SQUARE OF THE UFFIZI. - Vasari was commissioned by the Medici grand duke Cosimo I to construct this imposing building, which contains the Gallery of the Uffizi and was originally built to house the administrative offices of the government. Begun in 1560, it can be considered Vasari's finest architectural work. It was completed in 1580 by Alfonso Parigi and Bernardo Buontalenti.

Giotto: Madonna Enthroned

Simone Martini: Annunciation

Gentile da Fabriano: Adoration of the Magi

Paolo Uccello: The Battle of San Romano

Filippo Lippi: Madonna and Child with Angels

Sandro Botticelli: The Birth of Venus, below Allegory of Spring.

Leonardo da Vinci: Annunciation

Titian: Venus of Urbino

Michelangelo: The Holy Family ▶

Santa Croce

In the photo at left, the **Church of Santa Croce** and the square of the same name. Begun in the second half of the 13th century and completed towards the end of the 14th century, it is traditionally attributed to the great Arnolfo di Cambio. The marble facade is the work of Nicolò Matas (1857-63) and the bell-tower, in imitation Gothic style, is by Baccani (1847). In the photo below, the **interior** of the church, which has an Egyptian cross (or T-shaped) plan, and is divided into three naves by pillars and pointed arches. Typical of Franciscan churches is its fine open-beam ceiling. The church served in earlier times as the burial place of many important people in Florentine life. It became a national shrine after illustrious men from every walk of life had been buried there, and funeral monuments erected to attest to the spiritual presence at least of other great persons buried elsewhere.

Cimabue's famous **Crucifix** before the November 4, 1966 flood which irreparably damaged it as the photo below shows.

Vasari: Tomb of Michelangelo.
Cassioli: Tomb of Gioacchino Rossini.

Foggini: Tomb of Galileo Galilei.
Ricci: Funeral monument to Dante Alighieri.

Donatello: Annunciation.

Benedetto da Maiano: Pulpit.

Giotto: Funeral of St. Francis.

Academy Gallery

The « **David** » by Michelangelo. The Florentine Republic entrusted Michelangelo with the creation of a symbol of freedom which was to be placed in front of the Palazzo Vecchio, but which has now been replaced by a copy. It is a work done in the youth of the artist who was 26 years old when he started to sculpt it and he finished it in four years (1501-4). This gigantic youthful figure is very beautiful and its pride and virility, physical loveliness and nobility of expression · tell us how much Michelangelo adhered to the symbol conceived.

Two « **Prisoners** » by Michelangelo.

Michelangelo: Palestrina Pietà.

Beato Angelico: Crucifixion.

Beato Angelico:
Deposition from the Cross.

Beato Angelico: Annunciation.

Another splendid view of the bridges over the Arno. In the foreground the **Ponte alla Carraia** (« Wagon Bridge »), so called because it was once used by wagons entering and leaving the city. Beyond it the **Bridge of Santa Trinita** and the **Ponte Vecchio**, with its three arches. In the background on the hill, the imposing mass of the Forte di Belvedere.

The statues of **Spring** and **Summer** at the beginning of the Santa Trinita Bridge

The Ponte Vecchio

It is so called because it is the oldest bridge in Florence and was already in existance in the time of the Etruscans. The construction in wood, built in 972, was destroyed by the river in flood in 1333. It was then reconstructed in stone in 1345 by Neri di Fioravante who gave it its present characteristics with the shops along the sides. Originally these shops were rented to butchers; but in the XVI century, at the wish of Cosimo I, they were assigned to gold and silversmith: even today the tradition is respected a good deal. High up, on the left side, runs the famous Vasari corridor which links the Uffizi Gallery with the Pitti Palace.

The **Palazzo del Bargello**, built in 1255, and so called because towards the end of the 16th century it became the headquarters of the Capitano di Giustizia, or police chief, known as the Bargello. Today it contains the National Museum.

The **Sinagogue**, erected in 1872-74. In oriental style it has a lovely dome covered in copper and the windows are remarkably designed.

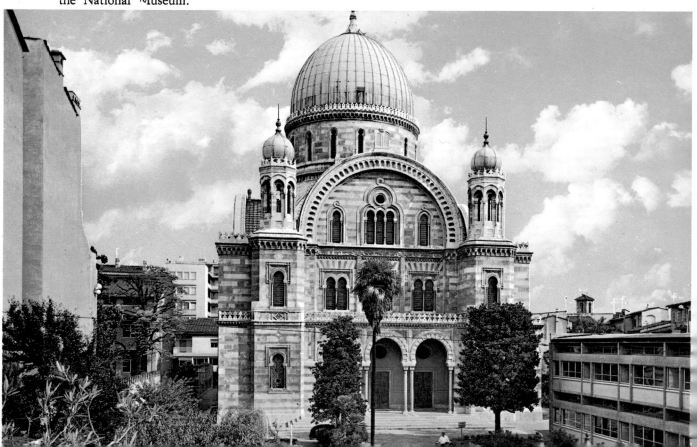

PALAZZO PITTI. - This is the most monumental of Florence's **palazzi.** It was begun, on a design by Filippo Brunelleschi, in the middle of the 15th century for Luca Pitti, a very rich merchant and rival of the Medici family who wanted a residence not only larger than all those already built in Florence, but one whose windows were bigger than the entrance door of the Medici palace in Via Larga (what is now the Palazzo Medici-Riccardi in Via Cavour). Brunelleschi designed the central section in the Renaissance style with its balanced and simple but imposing forms, consisting of three floors in rustic ashlar stone with arcades. Construction was interrupted in 1465 when the Pitti family was financially ruined. In 1549 the building was acquired by Eleonora of Toledo, the wife of Cosimo I, who commissioned Bartolomeo Ammannati to complete the construction; Ammannati's work, carried out between 1558 and 1570, respected the style established by Brunelleschi. In the following century, the facade was extended by Giulio Parigi (1620) and later, in 1640, Alfonso Parigi (son of Giulio) built yet further extensions, enlarging the facade to its present-day dimensions. The two wings were added between 1764 and 1783, on a design by Giuseppe Ruggeri. The building, previously residence of the Medici family and their successors, the Lorraines, became the royal palace of the Savoy dynasty during the period in which Florence was capital of Italy (from 1865 to 1871).

▲ Room of Flora. Room of Apollo. ▼ Raphael: The Madonna of the Chair ▶

RAFFAELLO SANZIO
N. AD VRBINO 6 APRILE 1483
M. A ROMA 6 APRILE 1520
MADONNA della SEGGIOLA

Boboli Gardens. — The Isolotto pond. On the island in the middle is the Fountain of the Ocean, by Alfonso Parigi, which includes a copy with variations of Giambologna's statue of Neptune in Bologna. Emerging from the water are Adromeda and Perseus. Around the fountain are statues representing the Nile, Ganges and Euphrates rivers.

The Fountain of Bacchino: renowned for the curious little figure which is said to be a portrait of Cosimo I's famous dwarf. ▶

Panoramic view of the **Boboli Gardens**.

Piazza Santa Maria Novella. — The church, designed by the friars Sisto and Ristoro, with its facade added by Leon Battista Alberti, stands at the end of this oval-shaped square with a garden in the middle. A famous carriage race was held around the square in the era of Florence's Grand Dukes. In fact the Medici Grand Duke, Cosimo I, had the obelisks placed at each end of the square to mark the limits of the course.

The Cloisters of S. Maria Novella. - The great Spanish c h a p e l : detail of « The Church Militant », by Andrea di Bonaiuto known as Andrea da Firenze (1366-68).

Piazzale Michelangelo

This is the most beautiful point along the Viale dei Colli which runs in a semicircle around the hills to the south of Florence. The huge square commands a panoramic view of the city, divided by the River Arno, and the hills that surround it. In the centre of the square is a monument dedicated to Michelangelo, with a synthesis of the most famous sculptural works by the great master: a copy of the « David » stands in the centre, and around the pedestal are copies of the four statues which adorn the Medici tombs in the Chapel of San Lorenzo. The monument was erected in 1875. The magnificent terraced square named after Michelángelo was designed and constructed by the architect Giuseppe Poggi in 1868. At the end of the square, on a wall preceded by a small garden, is the following epitaph: « Giuseppe Poggi - Florentine architect - look around you - this is his monument ».

SAN MINIATO AL MONTE. - Built between the 11th and 13th centuries in the Florentine Romanesque style, it has a splendid facade dressed with marbles of different colours. The upper part includes a gable window with a 13th-century mosaic above it. In the photo below, the **interior** of the church, with three naves. At the end of the central nave is the **Chapel of the Crucifix**, by Michelozzo (1448).

FORTE DI BELVEDERE. - It was built for the grand duke Ferdinand I by Bernardo Buontalenti between 1590 and 1595, to a design by Giovanni de' Medici. The fortress consists of a central building with huge fortified parapets from which there is a magnificent view of the city and the surrounding hills.

FIESOLE. - A view of Piazza Mino da Fiesole, with the equestrian monument depicting the meeting between Garibaldi and Victor Emanuel II in the centre.

INDEX